GROW GREAT WEED

Personal & Medical Marijuana Indoor/Outdoor Grower Big Bud Bible

Dale Denton

GROW GREAT WEED

DEDICATION

To all those who kept things growing.
It's been a long time getting to this point.
Thank you.

GROW GREAT WEED

CONTENTS

GROW GREAT WEED

INTRODUCTION

I want to thank and congratulate you for purchasing this book.

In the United States, the medicinal and therapeutic value of marijuana sourced out from Cannabis plants is well-known. Current laws have permitted users to have access to it for recreational purposes. These are the biggest reasons why a lot of people have shown interest in cultivating this plant for their own consumption.

In terms of practicality, it is best to grow marijuana indoors. There are several advantages of doing this. First and foremost, a grower will have better control over the elements of the environment on an indoor setting.

Secondly, the whole thing can be a rewarding experience for an individual. Growing cannabis plants is not exactly a walk in the park. There are many things that could go wrong but in the end, if all goes well, the fruits of labor will be sweet!

Currently, it is not hard to find books and reference materials intended for those who are interested in growing marijuana at home. However, most of these books are quite bulky.

Prospective growers like you would most likely want a material that doesn't cover 400 pages or more of topics. This is the reason why this book has been put together.

On this book, you will be given access to a simplified way of learning how to set up a home or indoor cannabis "grow room". You will be guided on how to cultivate, maintain, and harvest cannabis.

 The basics of the vegetative and flowering stages of marijuana plants will be explained in the simplest manner possible so as to benefit even a newbie grower.

The contents of this book have been put together to pave the way for your enjoyment. If you will find it enjoyable and beneficial, it is requested that you purchase an additional copy and share it to others.

Thanks again for purchasing this book, I hope you enjoy it!

This document is geared towards providing exact and reliable information in regards to the topic and issue covered. The publication is sold with the idea that the publisher is not required to render accounting, officially permitted, or otherwise, qualified services. If advice is necessary, legal or professional, a practiced individual in the profession should be ordered.

- From a Declaration of Principles which was accepted and approved equally by a Committee of the American Bar Association and a Committee of Publishers and Associations.

The information provided herein is stated to be truthful and consistent, in that any liability, in terms of inattention or otherwise, by any usage or abuse of any policies, processes, or directions contained within is the solitary and utter responsibility of the recipient reader. Under no circumstances will any legal responsibility or blame be held against the publisher for any reparation, damages, or monetary loss due to the information herein, either directly or indirectly.

1 GROW ROOM PREP

I.   Cannabis Plant Fundamentals

Newbie growers must have a complete understanding of the life cycle of the cannabis (marijuana) plant before attempting to cultivate it. This will give rise to success in growing the actual plant and getting optimal harvest benefits. All types of cannabis plants, whether grown outside or inside controlled environments require the same things: a medium for growth, moisture (water), light, heat, and air. Its life cycle is divided into four major parts. These are the following:

- **Stage 1: Germination**

Through a series of interlinked reactions within a cannabis seed, the process of germination proceeds. When air, heat, and moisture combine, this starts a reaction on the inner part of the seed coat. Such a reaction results to the rapid increase in cell size of structures within the seed. The growing shoot and root pushes out of the seed. The shoot searches for light while the root goes for a source of water. This explains why these early structures in the seed grow in opposite ways.

- **Stage 2: Growth**

The germinated seed continues its growth through the development of the shoot and root systems. The initial root responds to gravity and water and goes downward. Additional roots develop until a fully functional root system is formed. The initial shoot, on the other hand, continues to grow upwards. Additional stems and leaves develop from it.

- **Stage 3: Vegetative Development**

During this stage, the cannabis plant will continue growing until it has reached its maximum height and width. Its response to light cycles is shown on how fast it achieves target growth rates.

At this stage, it becomes apparent that the root system shifts to specialized functions. The main root becomes exclusively meant for water transport. The newer roots (including root hairs) push further into the growing medium in search of additional nutrients and water. The light requirement of the plant at this stage is high. It ranges from 16 to 24 hours of continuous light on a daily basis.

- **Stage 4: Flowering**

Basically, marijuana is considered as a short-day plant. It means that it flowers during those times of the year when there is minimal amount of daylight (fall). Indoor cannabis growers can mimic this season by controlling installed lighting systems.

The flowering stage can be triggered by making the ratio of light and darkness periods equal (12 hours: 12 hours). At this point in time, leaf production is stopped and the plant shifts its metabolic activities on the production of flowers. Non-pollinated female cannabis plants will produce seedless buds. Yes, this is what every grower should aim for. If indoor growing elements are successfully utilized, harvests will be profitable.

II. Plant Selection

The task of selecting which cannabis variety to plant is easy nowadays. This is because of the fact that seeds could be bought in online and land-based shops (in areas where marijuana use and cultivation is legal). Some people risk ordering online and have such seeds delivered to their doorstep.

There are several strains to choose from:

- **Cannabis sativa strain** – This strain is commonly found in areas near the equator. Sativa plants have distinctively long and slim leaves. These plants grow to an optimum height that makes it hard to conceal when grown indoors. It has concentration boosting and anti-depression properties. The flavor and smell profile of plants under this strain covers a wide spectrum. A grower would usually have to wait for 5 months or longer for sativa strains to reach the flowering stage.

- **Cannabis indica strain** – Plants under this category are said to have Afghan origin. Unlike the sativa strains, indica plants are shorter and flowers faster. If conditions are right, there are plants under this strain that would produce flowers in less than two months.

The indica strain has properties that will benefit those who are suffering from sleep disorders, stress, and pain. Growers just need to be mindful of the space requirement of indica plants. Although they have short optimal height, they can grow wide. Those who are aiming for the best possible yields during harvest season should choose this strain.

- **Cannabis hybrids strain** – In terms of popularity among growers, hybrids top the list. These are strains that come out of the crossing between cannabis and indica varieties. Hybrids are cultured to promote specific desirable properties.

There will always be seeds available no matter if a grower is aiming to cultivate indoors or outdoors. Buyers of seeds are advised to prefer those that are specifically meant to be planted indoors. Aspects of optimal plant dimensions, available space, and other growth requirements must be considered too during the purchase of seeds.

There are seeds that have been "feminized" already and these should be preferred in order not to waste time on growing male plants.

Plant Selection Tip: Go for strains that have auto-bloom mechanisms or those that aren't complicated to cultivate. Any individual who has no clue about which strain to choose should go for beginner strains. These include the following:

- ✓ *American Dream Strain*: This belongs to the Indica category but packs some sativa properties. The plant is grown for its pain-relieving properties. Many growers prefer this strain because it is easy to plant and maintain.

- ✓ *8-Ball Kush Strain*: A member of the Indica family which is known for its high level of potency. It can provide relief in case of sleeping disorders and muscular pain. Its earthy taste gives a user a reminiscent picture of top-rated hashish.

- ✓ *Afghan Kush Strain*: The power of this plant makes it good for those who have been using medicinal marijuana for some time. This strain is easy to distinguish because of its pungent smell. It has beneficial effects for those who are suffering from insomnia.

III. Planting Medium Selection

The "medium" in the context of this book is basically referring to where the planted cannabis will go. A growing medium supplies water and gas (oxygen) to the plant. There are currently several options when it comes to cannabis growing medium selection. Beginners who are aiming for little errors in planting should just go for soil. It is cheap, requires less maintenance, and is deemed as the traditional growing medium. However, those who are willing to take risks can opt to go for soilless types of medium.

1. **Soil** – One of the best growing mediums for cannabis plants. When trying to obtain the right type of soil for your indoor cannabis garden, focus your attention on the following aspects:

    ✓ pH level: It must be between 6.5 and 7.5. There are some soil additives such as lime, coffee rinds, and citrus peelings that could be used to correct soil pH.
    ✓ Physical composition: The presence of sand, perlite (sponge rock), and vermiculate is desirable. The soil must provide good drainage. This means that it must not be too loose or too compacted.

A grower has the option of making his own mix of soil or go for a ready-made pack from the store. Ideally, the soil must be composed of perlite, peat moss, and play sand in a 25:50:25 volume ratio.

2. **Rock Wool**: The main advantage of using rock wool as a growing medium is that it can be easily flooded during times of feeding. It also benefits the fast-growing roots of the cannabis plant by providing enough space for expansion. Growers recommend the use of rock wool that has been submerged to water with 5.6 pH level for an entire day.

3. **Expanding Clay Pellets**: These pellets are preferred because it solves the need for plant support and moisture retention in hydroponic systems. The pH level is typically at 7.0.

4. **Oasis Cubes**: The resemblance to rock wool is quite high. Those who are aiming for high yields for their indoor plantations should go for this medium. One thing that must be remembered though when using this medium is that the grower must always watch critical moisture levels.

5. **Hydroponic Systems**: This is the preferred growing mediums by those who have vast experience in cultivating cannabis plants. It consists of a soilless medium which has no nutritional value but can be flooded by nutrient solutions at

regular intervals. The growing medium makes it possible for the plants to get the optimal amounts of nutrient needed for growth.

IV. Container Selection

When the soil has been selected and prepared, it will be time to choose the container on which the seeds will be planted in. To grow the cannabis right, there must also be a right container to hold or house it. Containers can be chosen according to the mode of cultivation that will be used. It could either be through soil or hydroponics. Containers can be made or bought and even recycled. When reusing containers, one must not forget to sterilize it first.

A. Soil Growing

✓ *Plastic Containers*: These containers are deemed best for planting marijuana in soil because it prevents water stagnation. Stagnation or logging can affect the speed of growth of the plant. Commercially available plastic containers can come in a wide variety of colors and sizes. However, it is good to go for pots that are in the 1 to 5-gallon range. One must consider the optimal size and space requirements of the chosen strain when trying to select the best container. Most growers use the 3-gallon container.

For each plant, a grower must prepare two pots. The first pot is meant for the germination of the plant. The second pot is used when the plant is ready for transplanting. There are repotting guidelines that must be carefully followed and these will be discussed in other chapters of this book.

✓ *Jiffy-Pots*: These are pots made up of peat moss shaped into a bucket. Jiffy-Pots are meant to be the first pot for the set of pots for each plant mentioned above. The use of this type of pot eliminates the risks of damaging the root system during the transplantation process. Jiffy-pots decay and give space for the expansion of roots once the plant has been transplanted on to the second and final pot.

B. Hydroponic Growing

The hydroponic approach to growing marijuana will give good yields. However, the grower must realize that the containers will serve a different purpose here. Hydroponic growing systems are used instead of traditional soil-growing containers. There are DIY and commercially available hydroponic systems. Some of the commonly used systems are as follows:

1. Ebb and Flow System (Flood and Drain)

✓ <u>Materials Needed</u>: Plant tray, nutrient reservoir, timer, and submersible pump.

✓ <u>Main Mechanism</u>: The plant is placed in a tray with the growing medium. A submersible water pump with an integrated timer will be fitted into the tray. A nutrient solution will be pumped and made to flood the tray. This lasts for about 15 minutes and then the solution will be drained out. The whole process starts after another 15 minutes.

✓ <u>Pros</u>: The setup is good for both beginners and pros in growing indoor cannabis hydroponically. The system is easy to operate and can accommodate different sizes of pots.

✓ <u>Cons</u>: Incorrect timing can ruin the entire crop. In between the stages of flooding and draining, the plant's roots need maximum amounts of oxygen. Pump blockages can be catastrophic to the entire crop system.

2. Top Feed System (Continuous Flow)

✓ <u>Materials Needed</u>: Receiving tray, reservoir tanks, pump.

✓ <u>Main Mechanism</u>: The nutrient solution is pumped to the tray on which the roots of the plant are located. The nutrient solution is made to flow continuously from the reservoir tanks to the tray and vice versa.

✓ <u>Pros</u>: Compensating for problems that arise from sudden pH, EC, and temperature levels is easy. Plants can grow faster because access to nutrients is maximized.

✓ <u>Cons</u>: Power outages can ruin the entire crop. This is because the grower has little or no room for maneuvering in case such a problem happens. The grower must also take into consideration the aspects of noise, size, and modularity when choosing this type of hydroponic system.

3. Deep Water Reservoir System

✓ <u>Materials</u>: Deep nutrient container, tray for growing medium, aquarium pump.

✓ Main Mechanism: A tray that holds the medium and the plant is made to sit in a container that has about 2-inches of nutrient solution. The aquarium pump is fitted into the container to supply air into the roots of the plant. It is a common practice among growers to put holes into the tray and to control algae growth through sunlight suppression.

✓ Pros: The setup is quite simple and can be used by beginners.

✓ Cons: Noise will be produced by the aquarium pumps. The noise level will increase when the power of the pump is increased. This is why the power of the pump to be bought should correspond to the dimensions of the containers.

V. Lighting and Ventilation Equipment Selection

One of the best things about growing cannabis indoors is that you'll have control over the lighting conditions. Natural sunlight which is being used by outdoor cannabis growers is quite unpredictable. This means that as a beginner indoor grower, your chances for success are higher. Cannabis and other similar plants share this property called photo morphogenesis. Different light spectrums stimulate specific types of growth processes. Vegetative growth, as an example, is stimulated by the blue spectrum. On the other hand, reproductive growth is triggered by the red, amber, and yellow spectrum. Light wavelengths that range from 420 – 730 nanometers are needed for a cannabis plant to grow to maturity.

There is a need for you to emulate natural sunlight and this can be possible through the use of grow lights. Before going to the store to buy grow lights, there are some light qualities that you must be familiar with. These are the following:

- ✓ Kelvin – This is a measure of temperature. In terms of marijuana growing, Kelvin is correlated to the specific temperature that comes with particular wavelengths of light.

  During the vegetative stage of the plant's life, the heat coming from the midday sun must be emulated. This is linked to the blue spectrum which has a temperature equivalent of 6,500 Kelvin. The red spectrum which is needed for the flowering of the plant is equivalent to 2,700 Kelvin.

- ✓ Lumen – This refers to the overall quantity of visible light.

- ✓ Wattage – This pertains to the total surface area that will be covered by the lights. For example, the difference in the area covered by 300 and 150-watt light bulbs will be significantly different. The former will cover a larger surface area than the latter. For this matter, the spacing between each plant as well as the total area covered by the indoor garden should be considered when selecting the correct bulb wattage.

✓ Brilliance – The acuity and sharpness of light is measured in terms of brilliance. The distance of the plant from the light source can be used as a reference for describing brilliance. Growers must be careful not to place the plant too far or too near the light source. These instances could lead to the weakening or death of the plant, respectively.

Growers must choose lighting fixtures that are both cheap and versatile. Of course, there are many options available and the most preferred are presented below:

1. **Fluorescent Bulbs/Tubes**

   ✓ Benefits: These light sources provide minimal heat and are energy-efficient. Growers use these bulbs/tubes for both the vegetative and reproductive stages of the life of a cannabis plant.

   ✓ Limiting Factors: These bulbs/tubes don't cover the entire spectrum. If used within the flowering stage, the yield will be low. The bulbs/tubes become more and more unstable as they age. This makes it unsuitable for long-term use.

*Additional option: **CFL or Compact Fluorescent Lights** can be preferred over conventional Fluorescent Bulbs/Tubes. CFLs are available in the 6500 and 2500-Kelvin colors. Expert growers recommend CFL for small-scale indoor cannabis cultivation.

2. Incandescent Bulbs

✓ Benefits: Can be used to emulate sunlight and temperature needed by cannabis plants that thrive near the equator.

✓ Limiting Factor: The bulbs can give way too much heat which can kill the plants. This is the reason why this type of light source is seldom used by indoor cannabis growers. Additionally, these bulbs don't cover the entire light spectrum.

3. HID (High Intensity Discharge) Lamps

✓ Benefits: Comes in types that are ideal for the vegetative and reproductive stages of the life of a cannabis plant. Metal Halide (MH) lamps are used for the vegetative growth while High Pressure Sodium

(HPS) lamps are used to stimulate flowering. The cost-effectiveness of HID systems is also noted by many growers. MH lamps are in the price range of $84-$120. HPS lamps are priced from $25 to $40.

✓ Limiting Factors: HID lamps have a lifespan of only 10,000 hours or less. Current power consumption statistics also show that it is costly to use HID lamps on a long-term basis. There is also a need to invest in a ballast system or else there will safety issues. In addition to this, HID lamps could get extremely hot and might start fires if placed in areas where flammable materials are stored.

4. LED (Light Emitting Diode) Lights

✓ Benefits: LED lamps are favored by growers today because of its long life, high operational efficiency, and low heat output. It is possible to put LED lamps too close to cannabis plants and never burn a single leaf.

✓ Limiting Factors: LED lamps can be expensive to operate over long periods of time. In order to obtain a 400-watt equivalent coverage, a grower would need to spend as much as a thousand dollars on power bills. The quality of harvested materials (buds) will also never be as good as with HID-grown cannabis.

It is also important to look at what lighting add-ons should be prepared. Reflecting light is the task that must be covered when it comes to this matter. Reflector hoods can be used to increase yield. There are hoods that can be bought already set up.

The warning here though is that reflector hoods can increase heat buildup within the growing area. Reflective materials such as aluminum foil, Mylar, and white paint can also be used to increase yield. These are recommended when the grower isn't using LED lamp systems.

When it comes to the ventilation aspect, there isn't much to cover. One must just remember that no matter what type of lamp is used, there should always be an extractor fan system. Heat and oxygen content management within the area are important matters to be dealt with. A typical growing room or tent measuring 47"x47"x79" will have a total air volume of 2.86 m^3.

Under these circumstances, the fan system must be able to change the air every two minutes. This means that the capacity of the fans system must be at 85.8 m^3 per hour.

HID lighted growing rooms have more heat expenditure and needs more air. In this case, the work capacity of the extractor fan system must be doubled. This formula is useful when you are trying to choose the right fan for your indoor cannabis growing area. Of course, you'll also need air filters because cannabis plants tend to give off a distinctive strong odor while growing.

VI. Final Checklist

At this point in time, you should have already prepared your indoor cannabis grow room. In order to check if you have covered all aspects of preparation, refer to the following checklist:

QUESTIONS	YES	NO
1. Have I chosen a location on where I will grow my cannabis plants?		
2. Have I chosen and purchased the right seeds for my indoor cannabis growing room?		
3. Have I decided on what light source (HID or LED) I will use? Have I purchased the right lighting fixtures/add-ons?		
4. Have I chosen and purchased a ventilation system suited to the requirements of my indoor cannabis		

room?		
5. Have I chosen a container that will match the planting system (soil/hydroponics) that I prefer?		
6. Have I chosen a planting medium that is based on the pH, drainage, moisture, and nutrient retention factors?		

If you have answered YES to all of the questions above, it indicates that you are now ready to move to the next phase of indoor cannabis cultivation.

2 GERMINATION, PLANTING, AND TRANSPLANTING PROCEDURES

I.   Germination Procedures

Germination is the process in which the cannabis sprout will be forced out of the seed. Basically, the best route in germination is to place the seed in a wet tissue and transfer it to a growing medium. The germination process will require two plates or trays. Follow the germination procedures enumerated below:

- ✓ Step 1: Create a couple of layers of wet tissue on the first plate. If there is excess water, it must be completely removed.

- ✓ Step 2: Cannabis seeds are placed on the surface of the wet tissue. There must be equal and adequate space in between each seed.

- ✓ Step 3: Cover the seeds with additional pieces of wet tissue.

Any excess moisture must be removed from the plate.

✓ Step 4: Create a dark environment for the seeds by covering it with the second plate.

✓ Step 5: Set aside the germination setup in a room not reached by direct sunlight and has a temperature range of 21^0C to 25^0C (70^0F to 78^0F).

The setup must be carefully monitored during the entire period. Moisture levels must not be allowed to go down. This is achieved by gently spraying the tissue paper with water if the setup appears to be drying up. A root will break through the seed coat in a few days. In some instances, the germination stage will last from 10 to 14 days.

II.   Planting Procedures

Once all the seeds have sprouted out roots, the next thing to do is to plant them in a growing medium. Follow the following procedures:

✓ Step 1: Get your pots. Create holes in the growing medium. Each hole should be twice the size of the germinated seed. Put the seed in and cover it carefully.

✓ Step 2: Moisten up the growing medium with water. Take care not to put in too much water.

✓ Step 3: Transfer the plate in a room that is away from direct sunlight and has a temperature range of 21^{0}C to 25^{0}C (70^{0}F to 78^{0}F).

✓ Step 4: Place the plate under a grow lamp when the initial shoots become visible. The shoot will take a few days to appear.

III.   Transplanting Procedures

As stated in the previous chapter, there are two containers needed when growing cannabis. The first pot will be for the initial growth of the plant and the second one will be for the final growth and cultivation stages. When the initial root and shoot systems have reached stability, transplanting or repotting can be done.

One must remember that this process should not be done more than once in the life cycle of the plant. Doing so will result to plant stress which is a primary factor in development problems and low yield. The following are the usual steps in transplanting cannabis plants:

✓ Step 1: Prepare the second container. It must be filled with the right type of soil and is larger than the first container.

✓ Step 2: Dig out a space on the soil on which the transplanted cannabis (soil and plant) will fit in.

✓ Step 3: Pick up the first container and get the plant with the soil. The soil must be kept intact as much as possible. This is done by turning the first container upside down and sharply tapping the rim against a hard surface.

✓ Step 4: Once the plant and the intact soil has fallen out, it should be planted on the second container.

There are some tips that can be useful when transplanting cannabis plants. Take note of the following:

• Use Jiffy-Pots as the first container. This will ensure that the plant is spared from repotting trauma.

• "Root binding" must be avoided at all costs. Enough space should be provided for the expansion of the root system. Even brief instances of root binding can have lasting effects on the growth of the plant and the quality of harvest that the grower can get.

- The optimal time for transplanting is about **two weeks** from the date of germination. Proper preparation must be done within this period so that the transplanting procedure can be seamlessly completed.

3 BASIC PLANT NUTRITION, LIGHTING, AND MAINTENANCE

When the plant has been successfully transplanted, focus must be given to guiding it towards successful vegetative and reproductive growth. Knowledge about basic plant nutrition, lighting, and maintenance will be crucial on growing healthy plants and getting excellent yield. Fortunately, cannabis plants aren't that hard to cultivate when the right materials are used and recommended growing procedures are followed.

I. Basic Plant Nutrition

In order to grow to optimal levels, the cannabis plant must be supplied with the right nutrients. The soil on which it has been transplanted on will have the required nutrients. However, after three weeks, these will be depleted and feeding will have to be done. The feeding procedure involves the use of fertilizers or nutrient solutions.

There are three basic nutrients that are found in fertilizers or nutrient solution products: Nitrogen, Phosphorus, and Potassium. The "NPK" label on the fertilizer label pertains to these three nutrients. Nitrogen is generally needed during the vegetative growth of the plant. During this stage, good amounts of nitrogen will mean optimal foliage growth and development. Phosphorus and potassium are needed in higher concentrations during the flowering or reproductive stage of the cannabis plant. It will help in the formation of maximum amounts of buds for the flowers.

Feeding hydroponic marijuana plant is quite different from feeding soil-grown cannabis. However, the whole thing is not that complicated. There are ready-to-use hydroponic feeding solution products that can be bought out in the market. There will be no problems as long as the recommended feeding procedures for each product are followed. The general rule is to change the nutrient solution once per week. The pH level must be constantly monitored and water must be added as needed.

Fertilizer use is a critical process in cultivating marijuana. Since there are many types of fertilizers that are easy to access, care must be exercised in using it. Too much fertilizer can burn leaves and roots. The recommended practice is to gradually increase fertilizer when feeding. Even when most fertilizers out there have been marked "cannabis-friendly", there are specific brands that have gained solid reputation among growers. Currently, **Rapid-Gro** and **Eco-Grow** are brands preferred by cannabis growers in the US.

There are two modes of feeding: Soil and leaf feeding. Soil feeding is the standard way of providing nutrition to the cannabis plant. It involves diluting fertilizer into water and applying it to the soil around the plant. Leaf feeding involves diluting fertilizer with worm water and spraying it directly onto the leaves. Salt accumulation levels and overfeeding factors must be carefully monitored when using this mode of feeding.

The following feeding tips are useful for beginners:

✓ Feeding time is every two to three days when the plant is in the vegetative period.

✓ Fertilizer amount should be decreased when there is an observable reduction in foliage growth rate.

✓ Stop feeding the plants one week before harvest. This ensures that maximum amount of resin is present when leaves and buds are harvested.

II.   Lighting

Cannabis plants rely greatly on light in order to grow to optimum levels and provide a good yield. There are different amounts of light that are needed at each stage of life of a cannabis plant. Providing wrong amounts of light will lead to the development of a hermaphrodite plant which produces insufficient number of buds.

A. Lighting During the Vegetative Stage

The plant must be supplied with 18 hours of light (6500 Kelvin spectrum type). This lighting duration will ensure that the plant will grow to maximum height and width. Lighting systems can be adjusted to automatically turn on and off at chosen time frames.

It is a good idea to measure the distance between the plant canopy and the lighting fixtures. Setting the lights as close as possible to the plant without causing any damage will result to ideal growth rates. The best way to determine optimal distance is by placing the hand between the light source and the plant. If a burning sensation is felt, this means that the light source distance must be adjusted so that the plants will not get burned.

There is no general rule as to how long the light will be kept at the 18-hour cycle. Usually, this will depend on the preferences of the growers. If they have achieved the right height and width, they can stop the vegetative stage by changing the lighting cycle.

B. Lighting During the Flowering Stage

The flowering stage is naturally reached when the plant has developed enough maturity to produce flowers. A pre-flowering phase usually happens 6 – 8 weeks after the germination stage. The pre-flowers that will emerge should be inspected for pistils at this stage. Pistils indicate that the plant is female and suitable for high-yield harvest.

The flowering stage can be artificially induced by changing the light cycle to the 12-12 ratio (12 hours darkness: 12 hours uninterrupted light). This change in the light cycle will not result to the immediate appearance of flowers. In most cases, it will take about 1 to 3 weeks before flowers appear. Take note that flowers start to appear from the top of the canopy and downwards to the lower branches.

Flowers will continue to develop until resin production and calyx formation has reached its peak levels. This peak period is reached six weeks after the 12 hour cycle has taken effect. There are some varieties of marijuana that require special flowering light cycles. A grower must research well on this matter.

III.   Plant Maintenance

Cultivation of cannabis plant doesn't stop with feeding and providing right amounts of light. The grower must perform some maintenance tasks that will ensure that the plants stay healthy and are growing according to expectations. Watering the plant, maintaining correct temperatures, and controlling odor inside the grow room are some of the most important maintenance tasks that growers must diligently do.

A. Watering

Cannabis plants need the right amount and quality of water in order to grow optimally. There are three things that most new growers of marijuana are frequently asking about. These are as follows:

1. What type of water should be used?

The options here include tap water and distilled water. Tap water is okay as long as the pH level is between 5.8 and 6.8. This is the pH that leads to maximum levels of nutrient absorption. The tap water must also have dissolved solids that doesn't exceed the 140 ppm (parts per million) mark. Hard and soft water will not work for your cannabis plant. If it is hard, meaning that it contains too much calcium, tap water shouldn't be used at all. If it is soft, calcium can be added.

In case of distilled water, the grower must make sure that it has undergone the "reverse osmosis" procedure. Carbon filtered water isn't good for cannabis culture since it still contains a lot of dissolved materials.

2. How much water should be used?

There isn't a generic amount of water required for cannabis plants. The amount of water needed will be determined by many factors such as plant size, type of medium, and container size. If cannabis is being cultured in soil, reference points should be established. One must remember that water requirement varies for each type of cannabis plant. In establishing a reference point, the media must be watered until it is saturated. The time until the plant gets wilted must be noted from thereon. This should be the indication for re-watering of the plant. When dealing with hydroponic cannabis, the best practice is to always check the moisture level of the medium and water as it begins to get dry.

There are distinct signs of overwatering and under-watering. The plants are overwatered if the leave become yellow and curl up. The soil is visibly soggy too and doesn't drain up fast. Under-watering is indicated by the limping off of the leaves which begins to turn yellow in the long run. The medium appears to be dry. If the plant has been repotted, it is a good idea to check if there are pockets of dry soil that water cannot reach.

3. When should the plant be watered?

It is best to water the cannabis plants at the start of the light cycle. Since growth activities are highest at the first burst of light, watering the plants at this time will ensure less risk from drowning. Spraying light mists of water at the beginning of the light cycle is a good way to keep away pests. However, this is allowed only during the plant's vegetative stages and not during the flowering phase. Water temperature must be close to 210C (700F).

B. Temperature Maintenance

Make sure that temperature difference between light and dark phases isn't too high. A 10-degree difference is recommended. However, it is to be remembered that cannabis plants vary. This means that their temperature tolerance will vary too. Seedlings and mature plants will have varied optimal temperature requirements too. The temperature range of 20 -25 ^{0}C (68 – 77 ^{0}F) works best for seedlings when there is light. When light is turned off, the temperature must be in the 17 -22 ^{0}C (62 – 72^{0}F) range for best results. Matured plants can survive temperatures as high as 28 ^{0}C (82^{0}F).

C. Odor Control

There are two ways to control odor: Integrate carbon filters into exhaust fans and use specialized grow room deodorants. If carbon filters will be used, humidity levels must be kept constant at 60%. **Ozium** and **Zona** are recommended types of deodorants that can be used for cannabis grow rooms.

4 PEST CONTROL AND SPECIAL YIELD IMPROVEMENT TECHNIQUES

I.   Pest Control/Infestation Prevention

Cannabis plants aren't immune to sickness and pests. There will always be possibilities of virus and pest infestation. The best practice is to always keep the grow room as clean as possible at all times. Pets can be carrying vectors for pests so they should be kept out of the grow room at all times. Plants should be kept healthy by means of a well-fertilized soil in order to build their immunity against common diseases.

With the help of a magnifying glass (8x magnification or higher), a grower must regularly inspect the leaves, stems, branches, and even the roots. There are signs of intruders that will stand out. Most pests can be removed through physical means like hand picking or water spraying. In the worst case scenario or large scale infestation, insecticides should be used.

The most common cannabis pests/diseases and ways to control each are indicated below:

1. **Spider Mites:** One of the most damaging pests to marijuana. They are hard to spot but their presence is given away by the appearance of a web-like structure on the underside part of the leaves.

Mode of Control: Spray with water for three consecutive days. Water strips them of their protective webbing. This leads to their starvation once on the ground. In large scale infestation, the use of insecticides such as Fruit and Berry by Millers or products manufactured by Ortho should be used.

2. **Aphids**: Aphids feed on the sap of cannabis plants which makes them destructive to your crops. They are easy to find and comes in a variety of colors that includes red, yellow, brown, and black. Aphids usually cling on to the stems and leaves.

Mode of Control: Spraying aphids with cold water to knock them off the plants is enough to control them. However, if the infestation has reached high levels, there are commercial and biological insecticidal products that will work instantaneously on aphids.

3. **White Flies**: The damage caused by white flies can be the same as those with spider mites. They hide underneath the leaves which make detection quite

hard. If the marijuana plant is slightly shaken and a white dust that seems to have wings emerges, this indicates infestation.

Mode of Control: Mix 1 gallon of water with 2 tablespoons of vegetable oil. Spray this mixture to the plants two times in a week. This should be enough to control white flies.

4. **Stem Rot**: This is a disease that can be detected by examining the leaves and roots of the cannabis plant regularly. If the leaves are turning yellow and the roots are developing the color of white, this indicates stem rot.

Mode of Control: The diseased root and its container should be dipped in a strong solution of hydrogen peroxide (H_2O_2). Properly timed watering will prevent the development of stem root in cannabis plants.

5. **Powdery Mildew**: This can be detected by looking for white-coating on the tip part of the shoots and leaves. This should be detected as early as possible so that mode of control will work effectively when applied.

Mode of Control: Since powdery mildew is caused by fungi specie, a specialized fungicide is recommended in controlling it. "Meltatox" is a fungicide that will work right away when sprayed on infected plants.

II.   Special Yield Improvement Techniques

During the vegetative stage of the marijuana plant, upper branches become more productive. Lower branches receive fewer nutrients and produce less resin. This is why it becomes lucrative for the grower to have these lower branches removed. This is referred to as "pruning". Generally, not all strains of marijuana benefits from pruning. However, this practice tidies up the plant and significantly increases yield.

Fundamentally, pruning is meant to stimulate robust plant growth. It also exposes all the parts of the plant to light, thereby increasing production of resin. Even if cannabis plants have optimal growth dimensions, some will grow exceptionally taller than others in your growing area. Pruning would be advisable on this scenario.

Pruning is done by cutting areas where two branches are going up against each other. The top shoot should be removed when the plant has already produced three nodes. At this point, a grower has the option of "rooting the top". This means that the removed shoot will be planted in the soil in an attempt to have it grow roots and develop into another productive plant. If this is being planned, pruning should be done by doing long diagonal cuts to the stem so that a bigger surface area will be exposed to water once it has been planted on the soil.

After pruning, the plant will observably become bushier and less tall. This will result in better production for the plant.

5 HARVEST TIME

It is every grower's desire to finally reach the harvest phase. This will indicate whether the hard work have paid off or have gone to waste. Growers should still follow some special procedures during this period in order to ensure that the final product has the right quality (mellow). The last thing that growers would want to happen is to get a product that tastes like chemicals (chlorophyll).

I.   Pre-Harvest Procedures

The tasks done within this period are aimed on determining if the crops are ready for harvest and the quality of the harvested plants are just right. Each seed strain has a harvesting schedule which is usually shared by the seed company to growers. While following these schedules is the practical thing to do for beginners, there are still some things that they need do to determine the perfect time for harvesting. The following steps should be done for this matter:

- Step 1: Examine the plant's buds. When half or three quarters of the buds exhibit a dark color and have already curled in, it indicates readiness for harvest.

- Step 2: Inspect the trichomes using a magnifying glass. This step is done to further confirm if the plant is really ready for harvest. The trichomes must have a mushroom appearance and the heads are milky.

Once the plant has been deemed ready for harvest, it has to undergo the process of **flushing**. This means that for one straight week prior to harvest, the plants will be fed with nothing but pure water. The process cleanses the plant of chemicals and brings out the true taste of the strain.

II.   Harvest Procedures

The harvesting procedure is generally made up of two distinct parts: trimming and drying. To trim the plant, a clean scissor is used to cut stems that have buds. The cutting is done in a way that the budded stems can be made to hang individually. If there are big fan leaves, these must be cut too and discarded. The smaller leaves near the buds should be cut and set aside. These can be made into a hash later. There are two end products that should be collected at the end of the trimming phase: the smaller leaves that have crystals and the stems with buds on them.

For the drying process, the stems containing buds are hanged individually. Air must be allowed to circulate between each stem. Proper spacing between these stems should be provided. The room should be warm enough to dry the buds and stems. After five days, the buds and stems should be checked. If the buds are dry to the touch and the stems are on the verge of snapping, this means that the process is complete.

III. Post-Harvest Procedures

Even when the leaves, buds and stems have been dried out, the development of the flavor of the final product still continues. There are some procedures that need to be carried out in order to ensure that the quality of the flavor of the strain reaches its peak level.

One of the first procedures that need to be done after harvesting is **curing**. Curing involves collecting the buds and sealing them in glass jars. Once the buds start sweating out, the jar is opened and they are allowed to dry. After drying out, the jar is sealed once more and the buds are made to sweat again.

The jar is opened and the buds are dried. This procedure is to be repeated for an entire week. The jars have to be monitored for mold growth. If there is mold detected, the bud containing it must be removed so that others will not be contaminated. If the buds have an acrid smell, it might indicate the start of the growth of mold. Set aside the bud and dry it separately on the open.

The curing procedure ensures that when the buds are smoked, it will have the right flavor of the strain. While the procedure seems too laborious, it is not an option for the grower to skip it.

At this point in time, the leaves must undergo processing, too. It should have undergone the same drying process as the buds and stems. Leaves should be examined for the presence of a gland shaped like a mushroom. This indicates that the leaf is good as a final product. Those that don't have glands should be discarded.

Trichomes must be collected after this step. The best way to do this is to use the **flat screening** procedure. It means that the leaves will be pressed or rubbed to a fine silk steel screen. Materials that will be collected on the screen will contain the trichomes which can be scraped manually with the use of a credit card.

The collected trichomes will be the final product of the procedure. This can be smoked directly or used as a material for making hash. Hash is made by sealing the trichomes into plastic bag and letting the setup sit in boiling water for seven minutes. The bag and its contents will be flattened by a rolling pin. The material inside will be the final product which is a hash that can be smoked for recreational or medicinal purpose.

CONCLUSION

Thank you again for purchasing this super book on growing cannabis indoors!

I hope this book was able to help you get an idea about how to set up your own cannabis grow room, cultivate beginner strains, and facilitate a successful harvest.

As a beginner, it is normal not to get perfect results out of your first shot on cultivating marijuana indoors. It takes a lot of hard work and experimentation to get things going perfectly in terms of planting and getting good yields from harvests. This book and other similar resources out there should be enough to give you the knowledge that you need to become a successful indoor cannabis grower.

If you are in areas where marijuana use and cultivation has been legalized, it would be a good idea to consult some experts on indoor cultivation. This way, you'll learn faster. However, if you are on your own, just follow the tips and procedures presented on each chapter of this book.

The next step is to start setting up your own indoor cannabis grow room and apply everything that you have learned from this book.

Finally, if you enjoyed this book, then I'd like to ask you for a favor, would you be kind enough to leave a review for this book on Amazon? It'd be greatly appreciated!

Thank you and good luck!

Made in the USA
Middletown, DE
08 August 2018